SHANE VAN ROOYEN

The Narrow Road [archived]

Look and Live

Contents

Foreword

Greetings to everyone,

This book is written by Shane Marquin van Rooyen. A true inspirational book. The book was inspired by the Holy Spirit. Assembled through research, study, revelation in inspiration. The book is about our Christian faith , our believe system and how we have to put the word to act to our lives by faith. In this book I discuss the path of life, the narrow road. I write about the importance of the qualifications on the road, and how to enter through the narrow gate which is the gate of life. I write about what it takes for us as Christians and true believer to get to the narrow door, what happens after . God expect certain qualities and qualifications from us to enter.

Many other topics concerning the narrow road and the entrance will be explained. In this book we find love peace joy and righteousness, we find the answers that we were looking for.

This book is to equip our Christian faith, strengthen our weaknesses and quidence into the right direction.

This book gives us the assurance that we are not forgotten.

Acknowledgement

Thank you to Our Heavenly Father, my family and friends, every reader that supports the book, thank you to reedsy publishers, Amazon.com, blurb, draft 2 digital a
nd all other platforms that work with my book. Every library, school , church and all other denominations for appreciating my book. To Facebook and all media and social platforms. Thank you
May God continues to bless all of of you, and take you from strength to strength and victory to victory in what you do.
Shane Marquin van Rooyen

The Narrow Road Look and Live

I was lost, in a world of confusion, where I lost my trust and hope for life, a world I never understood at all,

I was trapped between the walls of sin and illusions in my life, I was blind in the spirit and I was headed on the wrong path not knowing where I was going.

I was always wondering "how will I ever get out of here" is it just a big dream and will things ever get better.

Too many destructions was effecting my life and I was focusing on the wrong solutions for the problems I have had, life was not making any sense to me at all.

Does it not ring a bell?

Don't we all, sometimes think about this things and feel disappointed for some reasons. We all get lost sometimes in a world that feels like nothing make sense anymore, not knowing which way to go. If we look at the world around us and the happenings in different countries than the questions jump up from nowhere in our minds and it make us wonder. Why ?

In life, there is this two tipes of roads, where we as humans are traveling on, it's almost like if one is living among the death, because nothing sink into the minds and hearts of people, I remember this scripture in Luke 24:5: The women were afraid and bowed to the ground. But the men said, "Why are you looking in the place of the dead for someone who is alive? If we look at everything that is happening out there in today's world,

then is there no reason that we might go afraid and worried
for the shame of the human kind, we are starring in the eyes,
at a good road but also a bad road, it is a positive side and a
negative side, a right and a wrong and everyday we receive the
unconditional grace from God the creator of everything heaven
and earth, to make the best and right decisions and choices
concerning our lives and this two roads which we have to choose
from.

The questions one have to ask himself is, Where do I find
myself in this journey of life? Where do I fit in to God's big
and ultimate plan? Am I on the right road towards my final
destination.?

This roads that we are traveling on somehow do have doorways which leads us to our final destination in time.

Death is one of the doorways which all of us have to enter some
time.

"Life " is the opposite doorway from death that we can choose
from, allow me to say to you that death is not the end of life for
us at all, but it is actually the start of a new direction to our final
destination, for us as humans, it may look like if life ends on
earth when we die, but it is the beginning of something new.

After death, there is definitely another chance to live, see
death as one of the doorways where we have to enter, but the
decisions for the life after death, to have life in abundance has
to be made in our lives on earth, before we die, which we still do
have the chance of grace from.

It all depends on the tipe of choices and decisions we make
before our time of death,

After death there is no way can come back to make things
right,

two destination awaiting for each one of us created by God on the other side, as it is recorded in the word of God, the one is eternal death which means you shall be lost forever, or eternal life, which means you shall live forever in a completely new life with God in heaven, heaven which means it is a place regarded in various <u>religions</u> as the <u>abode</u> of God (or the gods) and the angels, and of the good after death, often traditionally depicted as being above the sky.

"those who practiced good deeds would receive the reward of a place in heaven"

Yes, for the Christian believer by faith, heaven is a reality. And we as Christians have to believe it with the depth of our hearts and all knowledge of our minds and understanding.

Jesus responded and teaches us in scripture, in the book of Matthew He said,

Go in through the narrow door.

We must always be prepared and on the look out for this narrow door Jesus was talking about. He actually guided us by teaching and scripture to show us the right way.

What did He actually mean when He said that.

I personally think He was talking to us about Himself, that is why we have to make sure that before we die, that we are ready to enter through Him. Why Him?

He said in His word, I am the door, no one can come to my Father in heaven but through me. He is talking about His Father , who is non other than God, seated on the throne of heaven, the creator of all creation, including me and you.

That I believe made Him the doorway, on the narrow road, He teaches about.

After death there is no more narrow door to enter through. It is like when you enter in to the other side there is no more turning back.

And as there is this narrow door which is Jesus, there is also that wide door which stands on the opposite side of our doorway which is teaches(Satan), who's job is to rob us from where we destined to be, but I don't want to write about him today.

You see there is a narrow door where we have to enter, but how do we get there?

The question remains. The answers are all written in the book of Life.

Entrance through the narrow gate is granted **through believing in who Jesus is and what He came to earth to do for us**. He is the Son of God and walked the earth fully God and fully man; not just a good person who performed miracles. But when they did not know Jesus as the Messiah and had no relationship with him, they could not enter the kingdom of God. **Knowing Jesus and being known by Jesus is the key to enter the kingdom of God**. This is what it means to enter through the narrow door.

By sending his son Jesus **to die for our sins**, God is working to restore the radiance of his own glory shining in and through us. The apostle John captures this reality well when he writes: "See what kind of love the Father has given to us, that we should be called children of God; and so we are.

John 3: 16–17

For God so loved the world, that he gave his only Son, that whoever believes in him should not perish but have eternal life. For God did not send his Son into the world to condemn the world, but **in order that the world might be saved through him**.

Every decision we ever make will affect our future. **It's the decisions we make, not the condition of our lives, that determine our destiny**.

Yes indeed, and our real future and destination is not on earth, but exactly where we actually came from. Yet the immortality of the soul is often assumed , even in the words of Jesus, who says to one of the men who was crucified with him, **"Truly I tell you, today you will be with me in Paradise"** (Luke 23:43).

That tells me personal, that when we die there is definitely another place where we have to go after all. Paradise is a part of the heaven we have to go to. We as Christians have come to realize that **paradise is heaven is our ultimate destination.**

Paradise is mentioned three times in the Bible. It first appears in Luke 23:43. "And Jesus said unto him, Verily I say unto thee, Today shalt thou be with me in paradise." Here Jesus was dying on the cross. For me, personal Paradise is a place of blessing where the righteous go after death. As we await on the new heaven and earth, by the second coming of our Lord and savior. There has always been a separation of believers and unbelievers after death. The righteous have always gone to paradise; the wicked have always gone to hell. For right now, both paradise and hell are "temporary holding places" until the day when Jesus Christ comes back to judge the world based on whether or not individuals have believed in Him. The first resurrection is of believers who will stand before the Judgment Seat of Christ to receive rewards based on meritorious service to Him. The second resurrection will be that of unbelievers who will stand before the Great White Throne Judgment of God. At that point, all will be sent to their eternal destination—the wicked to the lake of fire and the righteous to a new heaven and a new earth . Revelation 20 and 21

Today's Life is important:
I know in today s life here on earth, are times when circum-

stances just get out of our control. The importance thing to do when nothing make sense is, tell yourself that it's going to be a great day or any other positive affirmation. Listen to a happy and positive song or playlist. Share some positivity by giving a compliment or doing something nice for someone. Focus on the good things,

Challenging situations and obstacles are a part of life. But the way we respond will determine the road we will take and the attitude we will have along the way.

It's all about our decisions, that we have to make in life that can bring us to that narrow door the Father put in place for us to be safe.

The other door He teaches and warned us about is the wide door, He said: The door is wide and the road is easy that leads to hell. Another reality for the reason after death, so hell is also is a reality. Yes it is, If you want to believe it or not, but it does exist. The Bible describes hell as a real place, just as real as heaven above and the earth below. (**Philippians 2:10**).

However, hell is in a spiritual dimension that can't be seen , but it somehow manifest in the natural life.

Those who are under the earth: That was a common reference to the grave. **Paul is referring to all the unredeemed dead who await their final resurrection and judgment**. In other words, this refers to all of the unsaved people, and it refers to Satan and all of the demons as well. The grave was not Jesus destiny at all, the grave couldn't keep Him there, but He went to grave with one mission to defeat death. And He overcome it, so that we can also be safe from death and have eternal life.

Look at this scripture,

The road to hell is paved with good intentions" Possible

meaning: 1)**People who believe they are doing good can end up doing bad** (the law of unintended consequences).

There is no value in simply planning to do good if you don't actually do it.

Many people are going through that door. Why is it than that many people choose to go that way if it is such a doorway that can cost our eternity. Is it because they want to live an easy life, although they know that it leads to hell.

Carry your own Cross:

The narrow road, I believe this is the right way,

The narrow and not easy way, He said, but the door is narrow and the road is hard that leads to life that lasts forever. Jesus says that the narrow gate leads to a "hard" road, one that will take us through hardships and difficult decisions. Following Jesus requires crucifying our flesh . When faced with the choice between a narrow, bumpy road and a wide, paved highway, most of us choose the easier road. Human nature gravitates toward comfort and pleasure. When faced with the reality of denying themselves to follow Jesus, most people turn away.

Jesus never sweet talk the truth at all, and the truth is, that not many people are willing to pay the price to follow Him. The cost of following Jesus is **everything**. He wants our whole heart, all of our desires, our own will. He wants us to put our whole faith in Him and Him alone. To follow Jesus means to carry your cross daily. To carry your cross, it simply means to **fully put your trust in God amid the storms and battles in your life**. It means that although you may be in an extremely difficult or painful situation, you always trust that God is with you in the midst of your suffering. As Christians, we try to live our life according to the will of God.

The truth shall set us free, it sometimes hurt, but it has the ability to bring us hope to a new life in Christ, God offers salvation to everyone who accepts it. This is the narrow door on the narrow road to have life and life in abundance, few people are finding it. , just a few people, wasn't it said, That is why we as followers of Christ have to make sure everyday of our lives, because of the chance of grace from God that we are still on the right path of life in order to follow Him the way He want us to follow Him. It is not just about praying and living my own life and going to church, but it is a much deeper relationship and spiritual contact with God. To believe without any doubt completely and to do what He want us to do. **Be willing to obey and submit**.

Christ's followers trustfully obey and submit to his will by faith, even when it exceeds understanding. "Jesus answered him, 'If anyone loves me, he will keep my word, and my Father will love him, and we will come to him and make our home with him'" (John 14:23).

To live in peace and forgiveness, love and kindness, the scriptures make it clear: the narrow path is Jesus Himself. We can not just proclaim that we follow Jesus, but our believe is in doubts and fear. We have to follow Him in all truth of heart , mind and soul by His examples to lead, love and serve others, and when we're told "narrow is the way" and "narrow is the door," we were told that many will seek other avenues to heaven, but the only road that can possibly lead to heaven is through Christ by His sacrifice for mankind.

We are all part of a bigger family, called The body of Christ and we have to make sure that we are leading our own families which are part of the body of Christ into the right direction, to find and understand the narrow road He talked about in scripture, isn't it that **For as the body is one, and hath many members, and all the members of that one body, being many, are one body: so also is Christ**. For by one Spirit are we all baptized into one body, whether we be Jews or Gentiles, whether we be bond or free; and have been all made to drink into one Spirit. We are social beings created by God and we are not meant to be alone. We need each other for many things, such as:

Caring, tenderness, hugs, touch and emotional support. Connection, sharing love. Learning and growing emotionally and spiritually. And we are tested on this road.

The narrow gate, which Jesus talked about, and we need to seek for it.

The process for seeking and finding does not start at someone else, but it start by oneself. As we search and seek I can give you the assurance that God is also looking out for us, but we have to come awake from our spiritual death to see it. Spiritual death is the **separation from God**. The scriptures teach of two sources of spiritual death. The first source is the Fall, and the second is our own disobedience. Spiritual death can be overcome through the Atonement of Jesus Christ and by obedience to His Words. Jesus is always searching for you and wants you to find him. In his own words, Jesus said, **"Ask and it will be given to you; seek and you will find; knock and the door will be opened to you. For everyone who asks receives; he who seeks finds; and to him who knocks, the door will be opened"** You have to make sure that you are seeking to find the door, so that you can lead those who are important to you with love into the right direction. Everyone in this world that we are currently ling in must actually be important to each other as they are for God, including your own friends and family. Is it not said in Proverbs 4 that "Above all else, guard your heart, for everything you do flows from it."

These words of wisdom from King Solomon emphasize the importance of protecting our innermost being. Our heart is the source of our thoughts, attitudes, beliefs, and actions. Therefore, it is crucial to guard our hearts above all else. **A good heated person produces good things from the treasury of a good heart**, and an evil weatherperson produces evil things from the treasury of an evil or bad heart.

What ever you say or do flows from what is in your heart. Make sure you are **embracing Jesus' sacrifice for mankind, believing he died for our sins and living life for him**.

God loves everyone, and all people are important to Him:

You may feel unloved and unimportant in the eyes of the world, but in Heaven's eyes you are so valuable that Christ came and died just for you. The "good tidings of great joy" brought by the angel on that first Christmas night was "to all people" (Luke 2:10).

God is rebuilding you

But I also like His promise in Jeremiah 31 ,that He will do the rebuilding — even when plans of all kinds shatter, and you're left feeling unloved. Remember your God is kind. His love is everlasting. And He is both the architect and the one to rebuild you — by the power of His love.

Love God and your neighbor

When asked which commandment was the most important, Jesus said, "Thou shalt love the Lord thy God with all thy heart, and with all thy soul, and with all thy mind. This is the first and great commandment.

Like I said, it starts by yourself, to love God , and your

neighbors, that is the importance of life that we have to find on road to love one another like He did, than we are in the position to find that narrow door, then we can lead to lead. Without love it is impossible to lead His people or even your own family.

Listen to this: The Bible says,

God is love, and without love, it is impossible to please Him. The Apostle Paul put it this way: "If I give all my possessions to feed the poor, and if I surrender my body to be burned, but do not have love, it profits me nothing." – 1 Corinthians 13:1-3. Can you see how important it is to find love first, on this narrow road to enter by Jesus, We can not walk this road with bitterness and hate and division in our hearts, but love must be the biggest part of our hearts. You can have anything on this road or in this life that we live but love is the most important of it all if we want to enter through. Hear the Word written in,

Corinthians 13 :1

If I have the gift of prophecy and can fathom all mysteries and all knowledge,(in other words I may speak in tongues of men or of angels) and if I have a faith that can move mountains, but have not love, I am nothing. If I give all I possess to the poor and surrender my body to the flames, but have not love, I gain nothing. Love is patient, love is kind.

Without love on this road , we are actually nothing, and nothing is not the thing God is looking for in us, we have to be something. How do God look at us? God sees each of us **through eyes of unconditional love**, and He loves everyone—it doesn't matter what they do, where they work, how much money they have, how educated they are or what they look like. We need to do the same. We need to learn to see others as God sees them.

As leaders in our counties, societies, specific parties and denomination i this world, as leaders of churches hospitals , schools and even our own households, whether you are a mother or a father, when we take this narrow path, **we demonstrate our exceptional leadership and prove we aren't afraid to do more than what is expected of us**. By taking the more difficult path, we build character and become known as uncommon leaders. This is what God want from us as Christians believers, to be a leader to walk in victory, to move by His grace .

In

1 Timothy 3 : 4-5 God speak to us about how we need to manage:

He must manage his own family well and see that his children obey him, and he must do so in a manner worthy of full respect. If anyone does not know how to manage his own family.

How can one be a leader of his family?

Once again it start by ourselves and under our own roofs. Look at this, Children are a heritage from the Lord, offspring a reward from him" Psalm 127:3.

It's helping children love and live for Jesus. "Fathers, do not exasperate your children; instead, bring them up in the training and instruction of the Lord"

Ephesians 6:4. It's diligently teaching the scriptures to your children. Raise your family in the Fear of the Lord.

In Matthew 20: 25-29

Jesus tells His disciples that leaders should not exercise authority over people. The "fear of the LORD" means **giving God your Undivided Attention**. Teach me your way, LORD, that I may rely on your faithfulness; give me an undivided heart, that I may fear your name. Psalm 86:11 .

According to the Psalmist, an undivided heart leads to the fear of the Lord.

Instead, whoever wants to become great must lower himself to be a servant. Leaders realize that serving others is the only way to lead with a pure heart, free of pride and arrogance. This road is a sacrificial road, we have to lay down all other important things in life. Understanding the qualities we need to have on this road, a leader, but a servant character, not to rule and practice Auto, but to stay in low position at all times, knowing who you are in Christ.

Look at the teaching of Jesus, On the narrow road is a narrow gate (doorway), it is a small gate, and narrow ways are harder to find than the wides ones and must be sought deliberately, or people will not escape destruction.

Yes the narrow road is actually a way to escape from destruction, but we have to be strong to go by the narrow road. Jesus makes it clear that we all stand at spiritual crossroads, and there are two paths in front of us. The wide path leads to hell. The second, narrow path leads to eternal life in heaven. It is important to identify the road you are heading to, both have it's own price to pay. The Bible teaches us many ways about this roads we are traveling on.

There is a way which seemeth right unto a man, But the end thereof are the ways of death. Even in laughter the heart is sorrowful; And the end of that mirth is heaviness. The backslider in heart shall be filled with his own ways: And a good man shall be satisfied from himself.

The Bible tells us there is the wide way and the narrow way. The wide way is the world and all its negative influence towards us which the enemy have influence on.

We all live in this world on the wide way, but seeking the

narrow way. If you can figure it out and see that the narrow way is actually within the wide way, but it is leading in the opposite direction.

So we have to turn from the wide road into the narrow one which go in the opposite direction of life.

On the wide road it seems just all good but it was never meant to payoff good at all.

What we must keep in mind is that, it is never easy to go on the narrow road, because the forces pulling against those on the narrow way are enormous, and it will take a lot of hard work and diligence and sacrifices to keep pulling along the narrow way and to bring along the younger generations and our families and friends, your children, grandkids, and other children, God has placed in your sphere of influence.

On the other hand,
the forces on the wide way may seems to be strengthen every day.

This means Christians need to be even more vigilant and diligent to do all we can to bring our families along on the narrow way, praying without ceasing to enable us to do it, in other words, recognizing man's responsibility and God's sovereignty and urge in salvation and discipleship.

What is the real difference between the two existing roads in life, how can we identify the two, the wide road to hell is easy, short and lazy.

The narrow road to heaven is hard and long, and requires discipline. Difference: The narrow road is thoughtful; the wide road is thoughtless.

We are sometimes so confused in life, about the two roads and we get lost.

One thing I am very sure about is that we often make the mistake to follow our own mindset and understand and it lead us on a road where we get lost. The Bible make it clear in : Proverbs 3:5-6 "Trust in the Lord with all your heart and lean not on your own understanding; in all your ways submit to him, and he will make your paths straight"

By leaning on our own understanding by doing things our own way make things much difficult for ourselves and it bring us on the not straight and bumpy road of life which is hard to overcome but always look like everything is easy to do, bit payback time is a disaster.

What does the Bible say about this narrow road that we have to find and stay on so that our friends and families could follow our footsteps, we call it His way,

The way of the Lord. When we find it then He is able to give us direction on the road ahead to go. Proverbs 3:6 - Seek His will in all you do, and he will show you which path to take. Psalm 23:3 - He guides me along right paths, bringing honor to his name. Proverbs 3:5-6 may be one of the most frequently quoted Scripture about God's guidance.

I know we sometimes get confuse about things, I know we sometimes do not understand His ways, and it is fine, but we have to keep on pushing, we have to call out again and again and again, until we find perfect strength in Him to go further.

Jesus Himself sacrifice His life to come and show us the way although He was the way.

On His way to the cross He trembled, He was down on His knees , He laid down to ground in His own wounds, scars and blood, but He did not stay in a lying position, He stood up time after time and pushed on. Why?

To show us an example to never give up , but to push through.

That road He traveled was not an easy road at all, He suffered to pay the price for redemption for living the Christian life, one that we still use today. By it, I mean that with every step we take, we are to be in obedience to God. There is not an inch of ground that we cover that is not done in the name of Jesus.

To be a Christ follower, with Jesus's beautifully detailing and describing "the narrow path." This path can be summarized as, 'embracing Jesus' sacrifice for mankind, believing he died for our sins and living life for him. To teach our children and their children and children's children the believe and the truth that can set them free.

Walking by faith means having an eternal perspective, so that we can feel at home in both worlds, Walking by faith and not sight.

meaning The eyes on what is eternal and not for a while. "So we fix our eyes not on what is seen, but on what is unseen, since what is seen is temporary, but what is unseen is eternal"

We look and we live in faith by His grace so that we can enter in through Him.

Entrance through the narrow gate is granted through believing in who Jesus is and what He came to earth to do for us. Walking by faith means living in a way that shows we confidently believe in God's promises, and this pleases God. It means we don't just read passages of the Bible for comfort or reassurance, but we trust them enough to change our daily decisions at work, at school, and in our relationships based on what they say.

Our believe on this narrow road we try to live on in obedience is through faith and we have to stick to the word day by day that teach us what faith in God means, Faith is, to Hear the Word, Believe the Word, Speak the Word, and Do the Word. Romans 10 : 17 says that faith comes by hearing. Hearing is the first step of faith. You must hear the Word of God in your heart. Paul writes in Romans 10 : 17, "Consequently, faith comes from hearing the message, and the message is heard through the word of Christ."

And when we place our trust in the word and act on Christ for salvation. Then we take additional steps as we follow Him throughout our lives. Oftentimes, like Abraham, we don't see the whole staircase, but we have just enough faith for the step that we're on.

As a household leader, which usually means a Mom or a Dad, an influencer of your family; it's up to you to create a place where all the elements of growth and the kids' work come together. If you are leading with integrity, that means you're working hard in faith with the right attention then God is working hard, and really good things will happen.

It is important for you to act by faith in believe as a role model to your family and hold yourself to high standards, such as being fair and honest and following through with commitments. Communicate and actively listen.

Use two-way communication without interrupting, and make your points calmly and clearly. Act wise upon His word.

I remember, how I almost failed on my family, but God helped me to become better and stronger. On this riad grace is always available, On this road no one is to bad to become better or even the best, but it is a choice we have to make by ourselves to lead well. As Christians, our children has to be seen as important gifts from God and we have to make sure they are trained well and equipped against the attacks from the forces on the wide road of life.Train up a child in the way he should go [teaching him to seek God's wisdom and will for his abilities and talents], Even when he is old he will not depart from it.

Can you see how important it is to act like a real role model to your children's lives, because they will definitely come to need for what you laid down for them.

So how so we train and equip our children and prepare them for what might come their way.

Talk About How Much God Loves Them.

Teach the Concept of Right and Wrong

Parent with Unconditional Love.

Talk About How Sin Affects Relationships.

Create a Culture of Forgiveness.

Raise them in the Fear of God and teach them the right way,

Lead by example.

Show them critical thinking skills.

Teach them how to love by loving them unconditionally.

Help them serve others.

Share your faith with them through scripture.

Pray with them.

Allow them to have their own faith.

But guide them by the Word of God.

The Bible advocates firm discipline, and certainly the instruction is proper in Proverbs 19:18, when it says, "Chasten thy son while there is hope (while he is small), and let not thy soul spare for his crying." And we are instructed further in Proverbs 13:24 with the words, "He that spares the rod hates his son.

Our children somehow get lost in this world not knowing what to do next,

One most important thing to start upon their lives is with love, show them as much love as you can, speak positive things over then and try to keep them always happy.

Training up a child is to teach, train, direct, start, and to give instruction to them. These are to be done, In the way he or she should go, how they should live, about his way, differentiating right from wrong, onto the right path, and the way appropriate for him.

The Praying Part on the road:

Yes its not an easy road, but it is a road that can be manage by God in obedience to His word.

It is no secret, when you pray together as a family, choose one person to say the prayer, and ask everyone else to kneel, bow their heads in reverence, and listen while that person prays. Teach the other members of your family how to pray, and take turns praying each day. There are many ways in which a family can pray together. One of the most important times for prayer is before meals, where we thank God for His blessings, and for the food on our family table.

We remember and acknowledge the word that says:

Proverbs 22:6

The Family That Prays Together stays together.

God blesses families who pray together, giving them increased peace, love, and harmony in the home. Family prayer is also a great way to help younger children develop the habit of praying on their own.

Once again, one of the most quoted verses about parenting is found in Proverbs 22:6, "Train up a child in the way he should go and when he is old he will not depart from it"

Cover your family on daily basis, cover your household, because the narrow road was never easy the attacks are real and it is heavy, that is why do not always know what and why things are happening in our lives, but He instructed each household to sacrifice an unblemished lamb, take the blood and put it on the doorposts and over the doors of their houses. The word atonement actually means "a covering." Therefore, when we plead the blood of Jesus in prayer over anything or anybody, we are covering it with the very life of Jesus.

Yes, It worries me that I cannot protect them from all of the evil in this world, that is why it is important to stay

on my knees asking God for your help and protection. It have to be our prayers every day to watch over our families when they step out the front door, and send an angel to guide them on their ways wherever they go and bring them home safely and avoid any harm they may face. Now we know, as God's people to proceed toward the Kingdom of God, there is a road they must travel. This road is not like a highway with all kinds of distractions, directions ,signs and warning, but it comes out from the highway to a small not easy at all road leading to destination. It's a road of total obedience, persecution and purification, and almost everybody who starts upon it will leave along the way.

The Bible commands us to pray for one another, "Therefore, **confess your sins to one another and pray for one another, that you may be healed**. The prayer of a righteous person has great power as it is working" (James 5:16). God manifests Himself in many ways when praying together and for each other. And it makes our lives journey more special.

How does it makes this road so special? I asked myself, The answer is actually very simple, because it is the only true road in life.

It might not have guardrails or streetlights, and it might be full of potholes and steep inclines we used to know, but it's the only road that will get you to your true destination.

This road is manufactured to be the difference in the usual life we started to believe, We don't ever have to be pressured by the fact that the majority of people do not believe in the Christian message and faith, but we have to stand upon it and grow on it. Jesus warned us in many times in thy world, that the world is under the deception of sin, they are believing a lie. We are to be the ones who walk in the truth. Only on the narrow road the truth is available and the souls of God's people can be saved by the truth.

Enter in :

Look at the question asked to Jesus, in Luke 13 : 23-24,

"Someone asked him, "'Lord, are only a few people going to be saved?'

But then we look at His answer,

He said to them, 'Make every effort to enter through the narrow door, because many, I tell you, will try to enter and will not be able to."

We have to make sure that we are going to enter.

MAKE EVERY EFFORT, to enter, so what does it mean for us as Christians? In simple saying, try everything possible to achieve it.

Do not give up on your believe, but try harder everyday, no matter the circumstances or the situation, but take prayer as a concern with you on this road.

"we will continue to make every effort to attract and retain"

The Bible consistently commands the Christian believer to be active, to be diligent, and to "make every effort" to please the Lord in conduct and character. Not taking our ease, but going all out, for God. There are many things in life that will not repay you here on earth, including the many times we are hospitable. But God does not overlook our efforts. He promises to reward us at the resurrection of the just for our hospitality in his name.

Philippians 4:13

One of the most well-known verses in the bible, but it's also notoriously misused. After telling his audience that he's experienced both poverty and affluence, the Apostle Paul writes these well-known words: "I can do all things through Him who strengthens me."

On this road, all things are possible if we just believe, and strength is found through Christ. God sees your efforts. Man looks at the outward appearance, but God sees your heart.

So God look at the heart of men on this not easy road we are on,

Proverbs 4 : 23

Keep your heart with all vigilance, for from it flow the springs of life. 23 Guard your heart above all else, for it determines the course of your life.

From the heart it flows, the quidence, and someone who is in contact with the heart to show us the way and direction which way to go next and whom quide us when we can not see on this road.

That is why Jesus said this.

John 14 : 26,

But the Advocate, the Holy Spirit, whom the Father will send in my name, will teach you all things and will remind you of everything I have said to you.

Our hearts have to be filled with the Advocate, the Holy Spirit, so that our hearts can work together with Him in His teachings which way, and what new direction on this not easy, but possible narrow road to enter through.

Together with the Holy Spirit, I believe work God with all His angels on a much higher level or dimension that we actually are traveling on, and we need to draw from it, The all known.

We sometimes get confuse and lost, but the assurance we always find in His quidence, Listen to this,

Isaiah 30 : 22

And your ears shall hear a word behind you, saying, "This is the way, walk in it", when you turn to the right or when you turn to the left.

Look and Live:

So we don't look at the troubles of the road, we can see now; rather, we fix our gaze on things that cannot be seen. For the things we see now will soon be gone, but the things we cannot see will last forever.

Timeless existence—being or entity without change—is what we here mean by eternity, and not mere everlastingness or permanence through time. God, in His internal being, is raised above time; in His eternal absoluteness, He is throned above temporal development, and knows, as the Scriptures say, no changeableness.

This is how have to look on this narrow road, without any doubt, but believe, hope trust and with love. There is timeless existence, timelessness we call Heaven, eternal life.

Ecclesiastes 3:1 says, "God has set eternity in their hearts." This means that all of us who are made in the image of God have an intuitive awareness that life does not stop at the grave. The Bible contains the most compelling and authoritative words ever said about life beyond the grave. Look and live.

Later in 1 John 5:13 it states, "These things have I written unto you that believe on the name of the Son of God; that you may know that you have eternal life, and that ye may believe on the name of the Son of God". Everyone who believes has this promise of eternal life, and we can know that we have it.

If we live, we live for the Lord; and if we die, we die for the Lord. ...

Just as the living Father sent me and I live because of the Father, so the one who feeds on me will live because of me. ...

I have been crucified with Christ and I no longer live, but Christ lives in me.

Jesus taught us the Golden Rule of life during His Sermon on the Mount: So whatever you wish that others would do to you, do also to them, for this is the Law and the Prophets. "Do to others whatever you would like them to do to you. This is the essence of all that is taught in the law and the prophets.

(Matthew 7:12).

In other words, treat others the way you want to be treated. As you do so, you will strengthen your relationships and be happier. Here are three ways to know you're treating others right:

be nice to everyone, don't say mean things behind others' backs, and treat others how you want to be treated. The Golden Rule says to treat others the way you want to be treated.

Psalm 16 : 11 David says,

You make known to me the path of life;

in your presence there is fullness of joy;

at your right hand are pleasures forevermore.

What a great verse and quote the psalmist used to honor God, because He found what He was looking for and he was pleased by the right hand of God over his life of Godly pleasures that would last for all eternity.

God takes great pleasure in seeing believers grow in holiness as He works in their hearts to make them more like Himself.

Philippians 2:13,

"For it is God who is at work in you, both to will and to work for His good pleasure." God delights in seeing believers walk by faith as His grace empowers them. Pleasing God can be mainly a matter of going to church, praying, working for justice in our spare time, and sharing the good news with others. To be sure, these things delight the Lord

. Ecclesiastes 2:11

Reveals Where True Satisfaction is Found. This verse shouting to you and me, not to spend our lives running after all the pursuits and sessions and pleasures of the world that will ultimately be found empty. We cannot hope to appease God by working our way into righteousness, nor sacrificing others for our own sin. Instead, Micah listed out the three principles of what God asks of His people: to do justice, to love kindness, and to walk humbly with Him. Live a spiritual life, teach your children to allow God's spirit to live and work in us,

knowing that our lives have significance in a context beyond a mundane everyday existence at the level of biological needs that drive selfishness and aggression. It means knowing that we are a significant part of a purposeful unfolding of Life in our universe.

Remember this and take it to heart, The shamans, healers, sages, and wisdom keepers of all times, all continents, and all peoples, in their ageless wisdom, say that human spirituality is composed of three aspects: relationships, values, and life purpose.

Where do we fit in at all on this road to live a spiritual life to stay connected and be guided on our paths.

Make spiritual growth a commitment and priority. ...

Spend time with God. ...

Live in the Word. ...

Pray in faith. ...

Have fun with other Christians. ...

Lead the lost to Christ. ...

Minister to others.

Spiritual growth can be spurred by regular devotional practices like prayer and attendance at religious and faith services. You can develop your relationship with your own spirituality by increasing your mindfulness, contemplating the natural world and works of art, and making things of beauty.

All the unique needs were divided into seven categories: ministry difficulties, spiritual needs, mental challenges, personal life, self-care, people dynamics and areas of skill development.

No one ever said it's going to be easy on the narrow road, but it is a possible road to walk on. The narrow gate and the difficult way

A narrow gate is harder to pass through than one that is wide, and only a few people can go through a narrow gate at once. Jesus was describing the pathway to life—true, eternal life—as something requiring effort and focus to enter. We have to strive to accomplish, BY "striving" to enter in at the strait gate, is meant in general, exerting ourselves with vigor, or using our earnest endeavors to that end; to obtain the salvation of our souls, or finally to gain admission into the kingdom of heaven. This is the proper notion and idea of striving, embracing Jesus' sacrifice for mankind, believing he died for our sins and living life for him. Philippians 1:27-2:4 Only let your manner of life be worthy of the gospel of Christ, so that whether I come and see you or am absent, I may hear of you that you are standing firm in one spirit, with one mind striving side by side for the faith of the gospel, 28 and not frightened in anything by your opponents.

Look and live, it's like we say seek and find.

The narrow gate is not a door that is locked, but it is a door that is hard to find, so some special effort is expecting, and some have to put in diligence and suffering. The salvation which comes from the narrow door is free to all, but it must be found, seek and find, we have to knock and we shall be go through, but nevertheless, The person who did not seek, would not find.

Many modern evangelists preaches and ministers have made out that salvation requires no effort at all, but it does, other than saying a short prayer and everything will be fine. They argue that any other doctrine would be "salvation by works". Definitely That is confusing the issue.

The fact that God asks us to search after Him is not the same as God requiring us to do special religious works. We cannot work our way to Heaven, but we have to seek after Heaven.

God is a complex spiritual and personal being to whom who wants us to seek a genuine relationship with Him and to love Him with all our heart, mind and strength.

Our souls belongs to Him.

True Faithful Christianity involves a true life-long commitment to God. In all works and deeds. Now the mind set on the Spirit mediates on scripture, sees beauty in nature, prays often and thinks on Christ, and looks for beauty and truth in all things.

The mind set on the flesh is only interested in gratification of one kind of another - from sexual gratification, to revenge. The road have to be a spiritual mind.

On the wide road it is all about the fleshly things, but on the narrow road it is about the spiritual things and we have to choose. The Bible describes the course of our life as a "walk" down a chosen path. That choice can be to walk the way of reverent dependency upon God in obedience to His instructions for life, or it can be to walk the way of those who deliberately turn from God and ignore His instructions. By acknowledging God in prayer and praying for Him to help guide us, He will direct our paths through the Bible. God does not speak to us through any other means, except by His Word. The Bible is the divine Word of God, and it is completely sufficient to direct our paths 2 Timothy 3:16-17.

Moses did pray in behalf of his followers, and in answer to his prayer the Lord instructed:

"Make thee a fiery serpent, and set it upon a pole: and it shall come to pass, that every one that is bitten, when he looketh upon it, shall live"

The instructions on the road cost obedience.

Obedience brings things to pass in our lives.

When we pray, we have to believe, when we believe we have to have no doubt at all.

We have to look at our situations on the road , but to live by the results of our faith.

All we need to do on this narrow road is Hebrews 12 : 2

Looking unto Jesus the author and finisher of [our] faith; who for the joy that was set before him endured the cross, despising the shame, and is set down at the right hand of the throne of God. Jesus is the life and the life giver. Without Jesus we are living dead but when we look to him, when we will become alive and be guaranteed "eternal life" (John 3: 15) and participation in God's Kingdom. Looking to Jesus means he is our reward. There is a parallel in this passage between where we look in our running and where Jesus looked in His. The text says of Jesus's own fore running: "for the joy set before him." Jesus ran for joy, for a reward. As our help, Jesus is the one from whom we draw power. He is the one who has given us life (John 5:21) and has sent the Helper to be with us forever (John 14:16). We run this race only because of His word and only by the power of His Spirit. So we look to him.relying on him. The word translated "looking" has the idea of focusing our gaze on something with confidence. "Fixing our eyes." Jesus is our encouragement in this race, both as our example and as our help. How do we look at Him and stay focused on the narrow road? For me this has meant taking time to pray, to dive into scripture and to turn to Jesus continually throughout the day so that he can guide my steps. Keeping my eyes upon Jesus means me turning away from a world that urges me to do more, be more and doesn't want me to focus on Jesus but on all the outwardly things. Whoever would draw near to God must believe that he exists and that he rewards those who seek him" (Hebrews 11:6). God himself is our greatest reward. And when we have him, we have everything. Therefore, "Seek the Lord and his strength; seek his presence continually!" (Psalm 105:4).

Hebrews 12:1-3

So let us run the race that is before us and never give up. We should remove from our lives anything that would get in the way and the sin that so easily holds us back. Let us look only to Jesus, the One who began our faith and who makes it perfect.

I want to add, that the most common reason why we choose to to look away from Jesus and rather die without him is sin.

Sin brings up the walls between us and our creator.

On this road we have to break down the walls of sin which bring division between us and God. Ephesians 2:14-16

For he himself is our peace, who has made the two groups one and has destroyed the barrier, the dividing wall of hostility, by setting aside in his flesh the law with its commands and regulations.

Walls(sin) can be seen as a source of imprisonment and division. They are often referred to as things we need to break down and overcome. However, when we look at walls in the bible, they are also seen as structures that protect, providing security, and represent a place of shelter forming a sense of belonging.

And Satan uses it against us to make us feel guilty. To truly turn from our sins and overcome our regular habits, we will need God's help. The only way to truly defeat sin is through the power of the Holy Spirit. Second, we need accountability. We need people we trust to help us walk through the temptations lest we return to our sin. Meditate on God's Word.

As you gaze into the glory of the Lord revealed in the Word, you're transformed into the image of Christ. You will abstain from fleshly lust, you'll kill sin. In fact, you will discover the sword of the Spirit, the Word of God, with which you hack up sin.

The Word of God tells you to guard your mind and heart. The hardest sin to overcome is the sin you deal with inside your mind. Mental attitude sins are sins you commit in your mind daily.

Romans 12:2"

Do not be conformed to this world (the broadway) of life, but be transformed by the renewal of your mind, that by testing you may discern what is the will of God, what is good and acceptable and perfect."

Five Steps to Renewing Your Mind

Step 1: Ask the Lord to guard and direct your mind. ...

Step 2: Recognize the source of self-focused and self-defeating thoughts. ...

Step 3: Replace self-focused thinking with a God-focused mindset. ...

Step 4: Rest in the truth that you are accepted in Jesus Christ. ...

Step 5: Repeat steps 1-4 daily.

To walk on the road is to me personally not just a personal relationship, but more like a marriage to God.

Marriage involves spiritual, emotional, and physical closeness. In the Old Testament, we are taught, "Therefore shall a man leave his father and his mother, and shall cleave unto his wife, and they shall be one flesh" (Genesis 2:24). Married couples are meant to be unified in every possible way.

Our relationship with God have to be like to cleave on to God, knowing that we can nothing do without Him and His ways. Jesus has a word about marriage, it is intended to be a permanent institution. The implication of God taking two people – man and woman – to become one flesh, means that God has joined them together (literally, yoked together). Hence what God has joined together, no one can separate , so it is spiritual to God.

Marriage to God Himself is a spiritual thing. Spiritual marriage means to marry your soul to the eternal love of God. Without God no marriage can be successful. The purpose of marriage is to know God, to be with God together, but this has been forgotten. Do not try to attract the opposite sex through physical desires but through soul qualities. The spiritual dimension of marriage is a practical source of food for marital growth and health. No single factor does more to cultivate oneness and a meaningful sense of purpose in marriage than a shared commitment for spiritual discovery. It is the ultimate hunger of our souls. Once again, But small is the gate and narrow the road that leads to life, and only a few find it." Jesus makes it clear that we all stand at a spiritual crossroads, and there are two paths in front of us. The wide path leads to hell. The second, narrow path leads to eternal life in heaven. When we follow Him we come to where He is now. Jesus calls this way "the narrow way." "Enter by the narrow gate; for wide is the gate and broad is the way. Jesus said, "I am the way, the truth and the life." Everything that you are looking for can be found in him. All of your questions can be answered by him. Don't look to the world for the answers you seek. Turn to him while he may be found. Whatever it takes, turn to God while you still have an opportunity. Jesus is the only way because only he made the way.

Only he gave his life. Only he rose from the dead. The Christian worldview is not one of many available paths.

Word of encouragement:

"Even when you might not always feel like it, you have the strength to do this!" "It takes serious courage to get on this path and stay on it. Good for you." "You have so many people supporting you on this journey, and we're here the whole way, no matter what."Believe in yourself and know that your gifts matter and that you are enough. Be simple, stay humble, care with love, hug with kindness. Power has ruined a lot of people. **Powerful people with a grateful spirit always remain humble.**

Humbleness is a requirement on the narrow road:

Truly humble people **think well of themselves and have a good sense of who they are, but they also are aware of their mistakes, gaps in their knowledge, and imperfections**. Most importantly, they are content without being a center of attention or getting praised for their accomplishments. Look at this verse:

A man's pride will bring him low, but the humble in spirit will retain honor." Proverbs 29:23

. "Humble yourselves in the sight of the Lord, and He will lift you up." James 4:10.

Of course, this is just a sample. There are many more Bible verses about humility. God gives grace to the humble. Pride closes the door to spiritual growth, but **humility opens the door of your life to more of God's grace**. To the humble, God gives patience, and peace, and gentleness. The fruit of the Spirit grows in the soil of humility. Humility is the key to spiritual growth. Jesus, taught them a parable and then said, "**Whosoever exalt himself shall be abased; and he that humble himself shall be exalted**" (Luke 14:11; see also Luke 18:14).

This is all scripture and we need to apply it to ourselves, so that we may enter. But **God will bless the humble person now, as well as in the future**. Only the humble person can be happy in this world, because we have many difficulties in this world. To be humble – in a biblical sense – is **to disregard all concern for rank and privilege and to live one's life in service to the least of Christ's disciples**. It is to accept all, serve all and prefer all – in Jesus' name.

So in simple text, Jesus tells His followers that "**Whoever is the greatest should be the servant of the others. If you put yourself above others, you will be put down. But if you humble yourself, you will be honored.**

We shall be honored when we enter the door with a humble quality of life. **When we live righteously and show mercy, the result will be blessings from God** (Proverbs 15:9; Psalm 23:6).

Whether or not those blessings are physical, they most certainly are spiritual. Our lives are enriched and often prolonged when we follow God's law (Proverbs 3:1-2).

It just makes sense when you realize that **God will bless you for doing the right thing**. Many of his blessings are obvious, but even if you are suffering for doing the right thing, 1 Peter 2:20 makes this promise: "God will bless you if you have to suffer for doing something good." God promises those who seek Him and place their faith in Him, are **rewarded with heaven when they die, and abundant life in the here and now**. Abundance for me personally means "forever". It means **when life ends here, it continues somewhere else**. The Bible uses the phrase in a positive sense. It is a quality of life that begins on earth and continues in heaven (Romans 6:4).

It's something Jesus gives next to which all other life just isn't quite life at all. Jesus invites everyone to spend eternity in heaven with Him. "Just as Moses lifted up the snake in the wilderness, so the Son of Man must be lifted up, that **everyone who believes may have eternal life in Him**" (John 3:14-15).

The Bible says in Isaiah 45:22, "Look unto me, and be ye saved, all the ends of the earth: for I am God and there is none else". Look unto Jesus today and be saved. **All the ends of the earth should look up to Jesus and live. It brings us to the point of believing with all of our mind , body and soul that,** Jesus is the life and the life giver. Without Jesus we are living dead but when we look to him, when we will become alive and be guaranteed "eternal life" (John 3: 15) and participation in God's Kingdom.

Numbers 24

Before leaving Balak, Balaam prophesied about the fate of **the Midianites, Moabites, and Israelites**. He prophesied a star and a scepter would rise out of Israel and they would crush Moab. He went on to announce future judgment on the sons of Sheth, the Edomites, the Amalekites, the Kenites, and the people of Eber.

Yes it was prophesied long before time, through whom we shall enter.

This means that **coming to Calvary and looking to Jesus on the cross can produce physical healing and spiritual salvation in the life of a person**. Therefore for anyone who has been bitten by the serpent of sin, if you look to Jesus on the cross of Calvary and believe in Him, you will live and not die. And when the angels at the tomb ask the women "Why do you look for the living among the dead?" they are announcing that the great problem of human history: **our misguided search for life and fulfillment, has been healed**

It brings us to the believe that there is no life on the wrong way, again it is like living amongst the dead.

Keep it together:

Children feel secure and loved when they have strong and positive family relationships. Positive family relationships **help family members solve problems, work as a team and enjoy each other's company**. Positive family relationships are built on quality time, communication, teamwork and appreciation. And that is exactly what we must have with God and guide our families towards the price .

Positive spirits in Christ.

Having a positive attitude means **being optimistic about situations, interactions, and yourself**. People with positive attitudes remain hopeful and see the best even in difficult situations. Look what Jesus said in **John 16:22-24**.

So with you: Now is your time of grief, but I will see you again and you will rejoice, and no one will take away your joy. In that day you will no longer ask me anything. Very truly I tell you, my Father will give you whatever you ask in my name.

So now Jesus again is talking about a day that we can be on the look out for in the future. Another translation says: **John 16:22** "So with you: Now is your time of grief, but I will see you again and you will rejoice, and no one will take away your joy."

Is it not true that , while we here on earth in this world trying to keep track , that you find so much grief and hardships, but Jesus make it clear, that it is OK to grief now, but a time shall come that there shall bee no more. The second coming of our Lord. **No one knows the exact time that the Savior will come again**. "Of that day and hour knoweth no man, no, not the angels of heaven, but my Father only" On this narrow and not easy road we have to prepare ourselves for that day. Because it is going to be a joyfully day of the Lord, and we shall be filled with overflowing joy from all grace.

Nothing else matter, we have to prepare ourselves and wait for this day in patients of faith. In the scriptures, the word wait means **to hope, to anticipate, and to trust**. To hope and trust in the Lord requires faith, patience, humility, meekness, long-suffering, keeping the commandments, and enduring to the end. To wait upon the Lord means planting the seed of faith and nourishing it

Psalm 27:13-14 says, "I remain confident of this: I will see the goodness of the Lord in the land of the living. Wait for the Lord; be strong and take heart and wait for the Lord."

Wait on the Lord:

Waiting on God **increases and strengthens our faith in Him**. We learn more patience, and our trust in God intensifies! Most importantly, we have God's peace knowing that when He does give us the "green light," we are in His will. There is not a better feeling in the world as we journey on the highways of life and seeking the entrance of the narrow door. Waiting strategically can cultivate good fruit in in our lives such as **patience, perseverance, and endurance**. It also draws us closer to our Savior and points those who are watching us to the gospel. Waiting in faith proves that our ultimate pursuit is God's glory. We can **ask the Lord to help us reflect his character in and through our waiting, knowing that he is listening in love and will answer at the time and in the way that will most glorify his name**. And this is always worth the wait.

- Waiting on God builds endurance. ...
- Waiting on God helps you pray and listen to God. ...
- Waiting on God helps improve your Bible reading discipline. ...
- Waiting on God helps you trust His promises. ...
- Waiting on God keeps you safe.

It's easy to let waiting distract us or pressure us to false-start before God says, "Go," but that's not what we're called to. **God uses waiting to test, teach, and train us for what lies ahead**. We need these periods to sanctify us. And by living faithfully in the midst of them, God will use these years to transform us. The process of waiting ultimately **helps us to be the person God created us to be before the foundations of the world began**. Waiting Is a Test of Faith: Waiting through hardships can really test our faith. Sometimes we are not just facing one hardship, but several all at the same time.

The Bible says in Isaiah 40:31

But they that wait upon the Lord **shall renew their strength; they shall mount up with wings as eagles; they shall run, and not be weary; and they shall walk, and not faint**"

It is important for us as believers and Christians to wait and renew our strength everyday. Since the effort required to do simple tasks when we are weary increases greatly, there is a tendency to faint or give up. But those who wait upon the Lord shall not faint, because their strength is renewed while they wait. Waiting upon the Lord is like resting in Him while He recharges our batteries. But, When we pray for strength, we may imagine the answer looking like increased capacities to accomplish or escape. But the strength that God supplies (1 Peter 4:11) is often **increased capacities to trust his promises**, which might require dying to our envisioned accomplishment or enduring what we wish to escape.

Remember: **For my thoughts are not your thoughts, nor are your ways my ways**," says the Lord. For as the heavens are higher than the earth, so are my ways higher than your ways, and my thoughts than your thoughts. '

The test on the Road:

The Bible tells us that **when our faith is tested, our character will grow.** Throughout Scripture, we see God test and grow the faith of some of the greatest heroes. Obedience seems to always be a key part of God's testing. He gives us things to do which make no sense to us and are not particularly appealing, although they are good for us. Then he watches our response to learn exactly how we feel about our relationship with him. If we trust him, we typically obey. Yes, we are not always obedient to God, I remember how I messed up in life, but we need to strive to obedience. **God tests us because he loves us dearly and wants us to grow in grace and in the knowledge of him**. This is why the Bible tells us we can rejoice when being tested. Count it all joy, my brothers, when you meet trials of various kinds, for you know that the testing of your faith produces steadfastness. When James says, "God tempts no one," the word tempt is the very same word in Greek for test, and we know **God does test people**. He says that God cannot be tempted, and yet we know that Jesus was tempted (same word) in the Gospels in the wilderness. In Matthew 4:1, the Holy Spirit drove him out to be tempted.

Things to Do When Your Faith is Tested

1. STOP! Don't panic! ...
2. After stopping, begin PRAYING. Prayer is the portal to God. ...
3. FAST. When we need to hear from God quickly and we desire answers directly and expeditiously—we must FAST and pray. ...
4. PRAISE. ...
5. Surround yourself with PRAYER WARRIORS. ...
6. GRATITUDE. ...
7. TAKE CARE OF YOU.

You see, God never tests you to learn new information about you. He doesn't need to "test" to find out something new because He already knows it all. Rather, He is trying to show you something about you — **to make you more self-assured and confident as you go forward to do His will**. He says that, after he's done the testing and purification, "They will call on my name, and I will answer them" Answered prayer comes after the test. **Before every blessing, there is a testing**. God tests you with stress before he trusts you with success.

Genesis 22:1-2 Some time later, **God tested Abraham's faith**. "Abraham!" God called…"Take your son, your only son—yes, Isaac, whom you love so much—and go to the land of Moriah. Go and sacrifice him as a burnt offering on one of the mountains, which I will show you."

And Abraham was obedient to God not knowing what is about to happen.

Abraham's faith was tested and He was found faithful. "One who is faithful in a very little is also faithful in much, and one who is dishonest in a very little is also dishonest in much."

To be found faithful:

I was never a faithful person, I was a dishonored man.

Trying to find faith. **God entrusts us with so much and it falls to us, as his servants, to be faithful with it all**. We can expect that as we are faithful, we will know God's approval and reward. "For to everyone who has will more be given, and he will have an abundance." When we're faithful to God it means that **we trust that He will care for us, we follow where He leads, and we love Him in return**. Being faithful also means that there will be some evidence of our faith in God. A faithful Christian will often produce fruit.God gives us the ability to be faithful:

He who calls you is faithful; he will surely do it." (1 Thessalonians 5:23-24)

"But the Lord is faithful. He will establish you and guard you against the evil one." (2 Thessalonians 3:3)

Just what we need on this road to be guard against the evil

one .Did you know that God rewards the faithful? For those who have placed faith in Jesus as their Savior will be given **the crown of life**. (Ref. Revelation 2:10) There are many rewards the world can give people, but there is no comparison to the gift of eternal life in heaven for those who are faithful to Jesus. The Crown of Life, is referred to in James 1:12 and Revelation 2:10; **it is bestowed upon "those who persevere under trials**." Jesus references this crown when he tells the Church in Smyrna to "not be afraid of what you are about to suffer. **The gift of God is eternal life through Jesus Christ our Lord**." (Romans 6:23) "For by grace are you saved through faith; and it's not of yourselves: It is the gift of God: not of works, so nobody can boast." (Ephesians 2:8,9) There is not one thing you can do to earn a place in Heaven. God not only equips us, He also works in us to produce that which is pleasing in His sight. The good works that we produce are indeed our works, accomplished by God's grace.

The Way:
   First,
   the "Highway" not "highways" refers to none other than Jesus Christ. God promises to provide a "way." In John 14:6, Jesus identifies Himself as "the way, the truth and the life..." **There's no other way (highway) to heaven or to God than through Jesus Christ.**   Jesus is God's Highway to Holiness. **You can enter God's Kingdom only through the narrow gate**. The highway to hell is broad, and its gate is wide for the many who choose that way. But the gateway to life is very narrow and the road is difficult, and only a few ever find it. You enter heaven by **forgiveness and through the righteousness that Jesus gives you**. You do not enter into heaven by the Christian

life. It's always true that where faith is birthed, works will follow, but salvation is by grace alone, through faith alone, in Christ alone.When Christ told people to repent He was telling them to 'change their minds' [which would eventually change their hearts] about what they were currently believing in works and deed [for salvation] to get them into heaven and to instead trust in. Three times in the final two chapters of Scripture, we're told that **those still in their sins have no access to Heaven, and never will** (Revelation 21:8, 27; 22:15). Hebrews 9:26 says with an air of finality that Christ sacrificed himself "to put away sin"

God forgives us from our sins, yes but we have to stop repeating sin.

There are six things the Lord hates, seven that are detestable to him: haughty eyes, a lying tongue, hands that shed innocent blood, a heart that devises wicked schemes, feet that are quick to rush into evil, a false witness who pours out lies and a person who stirs up conflict in the community. God hates sin, not only **because it dishonors him, but because it damages me**. Sin damages us, Christians. "God is a very happy God in providing gospel hope to sinners." Ephesians 4:30 says that we can grieve God with our sin.

God does not hate us as His people and creation l, but the sin we have in our life's. That is why we must stop sin. **God's forgiveness and love are unconditional**. He loved us while we were still sinners (Romans 5:8) and we cannot earn His love by our good works. We are forgiven based on the perfect work of Jesus Christ. God does, however, require repentance in order to grant forgiveness. We are forgiven based on the perfect work of Jesus Christ. **God does, however, require repentance in order to grant forgiveness**. Receiving God's forgiveness involves us recognizing that we have sinned and asking for the Lord's mercy.

We have to make sure that:

- Spend time praying each day.
- Serve others.
- Study the Bible.
- Share God's word with other people.
- Resist temptation.
- Put God first.
- Don't put too much value in material things.
- Trust God's plan.

Yes spend time in prayer with God.

Although there are no biblical directions about this, a reasonable place to start might be **thirty minutes a day**, half spent reading Scripture and half in actual prayer. Once that becomes an established pattern, increasing to one hour a day would be a good goal. This should grow out of an increasing desire for God. Prayer is important **because it's communicating**.

It is and has always been His desire to share His thoughts with us, His promises, His guidance. If you desire to communicate with our Lord, prayer is necessary. Then God blessed them and said, "Be fruitful and multiply (Genesis 1:28). This **makes disciples into disciple-makers and then forms other disciples also into disciple-makers**. This is spiritual multiplication. If you were to become a great evangelist, you might have the opportunity to bring many to Jesus. You could personally evangelize the crowds of those around you and heaven would rejoice. And much can be saved on this road.

Serve other on the narrow road you on. Once again, My command is this: said the Jesus, **Love each other as I have loved you**. Greater love has no one than this: to lay down one's life for one's friends." You, my brothers and sisters, were called to be free. But do not use your freedom to indulge the flesh; rather, serve one another humbly in love. Serving one another like Christ served involves **treating others with honor and respect**. **Take Time to Listen**. It's easy to assume we know what's best for others and to simply give them that material thing. But, if we seek to serve others well, the best thing we can do is take the time to get to know people and honor them with a listening ear.

Another thing that is very important to us as believers is the Word of God itself. We need to study the Bible.

Pray and read, to stay connected with Holy Spirit, to receive revelation to encourage others on the road. Since the Bible is God's Word, **studying it is a way to know God better**. Through His words we come to know not only the nature and attributes of God, but we also come to understand His plan for each of us. In a larger sense, we also come to know God's plan in history, His sovereignty, His providence, His love and more. "And how from infancy you have known the Holy Scriptures, which are able to make you wise for salvation through faith in Christ Jesus" (2 Timothy 3:15).

Bible study will help to reinforce the truth that Christ is to be the focal point of our faith. The Bible is also full of wisdom for daily living. **It teaches us how to treat other people, how to handle our fears and sorrows, how to get our priorities straight. It allows you to get to know God and have a deeper relationship with him,**

Yes we have to serve other people on this road, but we also have to share His word. Sharing the word of God is **an act of love for God and others**. It also helps us to connect more fully with our own faith. Inviting others to church or small groups, sharing Scripture and faith-based books, and telling our own stories are all effective ways to share the Gospel.

Matthew 28:19-20, It's a command that Jesus set out for us: to be the catalyst for eternal heart change in our neighbors and throughout the world as we share God's Word with others.

Romans 10:14 says, "How, then, can they call on him they have not believed in? And how can they preach unless they are sent? See the importance of sharing, It is a Command From Jesus

Listen here,

He sent them out two by two to spread the Gospel, bringing healing of mind, body, and spirit to those who received it. (Mark 6: 7-13.) Jesus wants us to share the Gospel with others **to bring healing and peace to them**, as well. **Pray before, after and during the conversation. Ask the Spirit to help you to have the right words to say and that your words will be saturated in love**.

On this narrow and not easy road, is it very important to be equip by the power of the Holy Spirit to resist the devil and all his temptations. Once again Temptation triggers guilt in our personal lives when we cave in to desires. Common temptations include **eating too much, spending too much, laziness, venting on social media, gossiping, feeling jealous, viewing pornography, lying or cheating and abusing alcohol**.

For the purposes of this article, we will define temptation based on the Bible as **anything that influences you to disobey God**. Truly any situation you face in life will either promote your growth or promote your destruction. The determining factor is what you decide in your heart to do.Temptation in the Biblical sense is **a situation in which one experiences a challenge to choose between fidelity and infidelity to one's obligations toward God.** The Bible declares that **the devil is the source of all temptation and is called the "tempter." (Matthew 4:3).** But he is able to succeed because we let him , and we let him succeed because of our own weakness and sinfulness. We want what seems pleasurable without counting the cost. We should not dwell on temptations. I like and I love this verse in the bible , because this was the same verse I took to heart when I was in a tempted situation.

James 4:7

Submit yourselves, then, to God. Resist the devil, and he will flee from you. Come near to God and he will come near to you. Wash your hands, you sinners, and purify your hearts, you double-minded.

This is preaching, you have to submit to God, surrendering to walk in His commandments illustrates our love for Him. Jesus said we will be blessed when we obey or "keep" His Word.

Another way we submit to God is by **responding rightly to the indwelling Holy Spirit**. We submit to being filled by the Spirit (Ephesians 5:18)

When we submit, then we can step the leader to resist .

Resist the devil, one key to resisting temptation is **consistent obedience**. If you give in sometimes, the temptation is harder to resist in the future. If you resist consistently, you get stronger and it is easier to resist in the future. Much of the strength to resist comes from the Savior's Atonement working in your life. I want you to take this to mind and be equip, devils **feed on the fear that humans and other creatures have towards that concept,**

gaining their strength from it. Because of this, a devil's power is deeply related to how humans perceive the concept and the visual images that their "name" inspire.

The road we are on is not easy but it is possible to succeed and enter our true destiny .

The next level is the most important fact of our faith in Christ, ALWAYS PUT GOD FIRST, ABOVE ANYTHING ELSE. When God is placed first and foremost in our lives, **we will be able to better live our lives for Him**. As Christians, we should want to live our lives for God since He has extended such grace, compassion, and love to us. The Holy Spirit can help us live our lives to God by walking in His steps. God's guidance is a great blessing of putting God first. The Creator and Sustainer of all things is the only one that knows where our path should go. When we put Him first, His guidance is a benefit that is incomparable to what we can do for ourselves or within our own strength. Putting God first means **serving Him with everything we have in whatever situation we're in**. It means allowing His love for us to overflow into the lives of the people around us. The same is true when we put God first in our lives. Holding God as our priority means focusing on God throughout the day and giving Him much of our time. Some examples of engaging with God include: prayer, attending church, participating in a Bible study group, or simply soaking up Scripture.It seems that everyone has trouble putting God first and keeping God first in their lives. We live in the flesh which naturally draws us into ourselves to maintain comfort.

We are to acknowledge God in all our ways. This means that **every action we take and decision we make should be done with God at the center**. God must hold the place of highest importance, and the way we live should reflect this reality. Zechariah reminds us that God cares deeply about true justice, showing mercy and compassion to one another, and not oppressing the marginalized or plotting evil against each other. **God cares about how we treat one another more than our religious observances**.

Our blindness for the spiritual gifts on the road:
What is the things that blind us so easy and keep us from entering in.

Sin is absolutely one of the things, but what about our material desires in life? Does God say anything about it?

So what do I mean by "material things" anyway? Material things are exactly what they sound like – they are **physical possessions that we acquire, usually by purchasing them**. Material things can mean anything from houses and cars to books or jewelry. It can mean your wine collection or a fancy dinner on the town. Anything that is offer to us from the world perspective. Materialism **prevents or destroys our spiritual life**.Jesus rebuked the Laodicean Christians because although they were materially wealthy, they were desperately poor in the things of God (Revelation 3:17-18). Materialism blinds us to our own spiritual poverty. It is a fruitless attempt to find meaning outside of God.

Matthew 6:19-34"Do not lay up for yourselves treasures on earth, where moth and rust destroy and where thieves break in and steal; but lay up for yourselves treasures in heaven, where neither moth nor rust destroys and where thieves do not break in and steal. For where your treasure is, there your heart will be also. Does Jesus warned us here,

It brings us to the knowledge that the material things could take our focus from the real price ahead of us.

The power this influence of material things have is on us can in some way destroy our destiny in Christ, materialism has been shown to **ruin people's relationships, increase a person's depression and anxiety levels, and make a person less satisfied with their lives as a whole**. Individuals with high materialistic values will turn to their possessions to find happiness, instead of turning to other people and can **destroys our spiritual life**.

Look at how Jesus describes the way we have to walk in faith in, Luke 12:20-31 **"So is he who lays up treasure for himself, and is not rich toward God**." Then He said to His disciples, "Therefore I say to you, do not worry about your life, what you will eat; nor about the body, what you will put on. Life is more than food, and the body is more than clothing. It has been observed that material possessions **bring happiness**, which is very short-lived. This is also known as "instant gratification", which soon fades away and once it does, you no longer feel attached to those things; in fact, at times you start feeling depressed and gloomy. **God may give us accumulated wealth**, and give us the power to enjoy those gifts , a great blessing (Ecclesiastes 5:19, Proverbs 10:22).

God may give us possessions, but through future persecution, he may take all those possessions away from us in the end (Hebrews 10:34).

And if you did receive it, why do you boast as though you did not?" (1 Corinthians 4:7). Paul tells Timothy, "**Command those who are rich in this present world not to be arrogant**"

Listen here, The New Testament never describes blessing in terms of material prosperity or possessions. In fact, it says just the opposite. We learn that God blesses the poor. In Luke 6 Jesus says, "Blessed are you who are poor, for yours is the kingdom of God" **To be shown mercy by a Holy God, to know His grace and love in our lives, to know God in an intimate relationship**

— These are true blessings.

On this road we need to be careful in what and how we believe and take to heart. If you want to let the Holy Spirit lead your life and walk by the Spirit, it's a conscious choice you need to make each and every day. **Pray that the Lord will fill you with His Spirit. Pray that you would walk by the Spirit. Then be ready to obey!**

Trust God's perfect Plan:

SomethingI have struggled a lot on my journey, until God revealed His great and altimate plan for my life to me. It was never easy in my life to figure it out,

God's ultimate goal for every human being is **to become one with Him through Christ Jesus,** to reunite with God in Spirit, to restore our broken relationship with Him due to sin. In other words, we were created in the image of God to live in complete harmony with God and God seeks to restore that, and lead us to all eternity. God, our loving Heavenly Father, wants us to find happiness and joy. **He created a plan for us to grow, live by faith, and return to live with Him someday**. His plan gives meaning and context to our life here on earth and answers the big questions: "Where did I come from?" "Why am I here?" and "What happens after I die?" and if you ever came up to this questions in your life than there is hope, because you are starting to get awake in spirit.

Some people don't think about this questions at all. Scripture repeatedly teaches us that God's ultimate goal for our lives is **to become like Christ**, to trust is **to believe in the reliability, truth, ability or strength of something**. So, when it comes to trusting God, that means believing in His reliability, His Word, His ability and His strength. The Bible says that God cannot lie.

That He always keeps His promises. That He loves you and has good in store for you. It brings us to trust and believe,

Romans 8:28 "We know that God works all things together for good for the ones who love God, for those who are called according to his purpose." The Good News: We may not understand God's big plan, but we should trust that He has one for us. Everything in our lives happens that way for His reason.

Romans 8:28

God knows everything we are going through at this very moment and everything we will go through in the future. He knows the best way to handle every situation so we get the best possible outcome and we need to trust him with that. We need to follow his path and trust that he knows best, because he does. Let me just remind you, trusting in God is a choice to turn to Him in prayer when we need help, and knowing that **God will bring great blessings into our lives**. God is powerful and good; he can bless us with things we could never earn or achieve on our own. Another reason we can struggle to trust God is that **we have limited understanding**. We see so little when it comes to human history. It is hard for us to know how suffering fits in with God's good plan. We are taught to believe that God's plan is good and right, but it's difficult to see that when things are difficult. **Spend focused time in prayer**. The most obvious answer to the question, "How can I know God's will for my life?" is to ask Him. Turn to God in prayer and ask Him what He wants you to do. God wants you to go through the process of seeking His will without believing the lie that He is trying to hide it from you. Throughout scripture God's desire is the redemption of all mankind. It is for the people of God to have fellowship and eternal life with Him. God's plan for you is the same; it is **to prosper and grow spiritually in Christ**.

His plan to give you a hope and future has never changed. Trusting God is an essential element of true and saving faith that **looks to God and finds peace, strength, contentment, and much more in him, and all that he has done, is doing, and will do, both now and forever in his Son Jesus Christ**.

Strength:

Is very, very important every day of our traveling journey before we enter. Without strength we will not make it, strength comes from God through Jesus,

Isaiah 41:10, "So do not fear, for I am with you; do not be dismayed, for I am your God. I will strengthen you and help you; I will uphold you with my righteous right hand." Fear can overtake us, but God is all-powerful and will offer us all the strength we need. In **2 Corinthians 12**, Paul quotes Jesus who said, "My grace is sufficient for you, for my power is made perfect in weakness." God is perfect in every way, giving Him the power to make up for any weaknesses we have. Pray for strength everyday.

Exodus 15:2

The Lord is my strength and my defense; he has become my salvation. He is my God, and I will praise him, my father's God, and I will exalt him. In every season, God is our greatest source of strength. He is our defender, our salvation, and is good and faithful in every way.

On the this road we are surrounded the dark, although we can not see it with the physical eye, because God has lightened us our eyes for the real dark territory, but we need His guidance, Guided by God's word **Psalm 119:105**

Your word is a lamp for my feet, a light on my path. The psalmist calls Scripture a lamp for his feet and a light on his path.

By reading, memorizing, and meditating on God's Word, the psalmist feels better equipped to understand the course before him and to avoid getting lost.

We must never stop to read , memorize, or meditate on God's word, it is our light in this dark world.

Prayer:

Thank you, Lord, for your new beginnings and unwavering provision. I trust that your peace will watch over me as I step into a new beginning. This year, I will rely on the riches of your love and grace to provide for my physical, emotional and spiritual needs. In Jesus' name, Amen.

Start over:

God sees all of time from beginning to end, and He tells us the same thing He told Israel back then: "Forget the former things, do not dwell on the past. See, I am doing a new thing!" (**Isaiah 43:18-19**). Starting over is never easy. But give your concerns to the Lord.

The spiritual meaning of new beginnings is **a time to start over, to begin again**. It's the perfect chance to clean the slate, put the past behind us, and move forward with a clear conscience. New beginnings are significant because they offer a chance to break with the old and give hope for the future.God doesn't remember our past, he gives us a fresh start.**What is a good Bible verse for new beginnings?**

Jeremiah 29 ''For I know the plans I have for you,' declares the LORD, 'plans to prosper you and not to harm you, plans to give you hope and a future. '" This is one of the most powerful

Bible verses about new beginnings. Repentance , It means three things: First, **take responsibility for your sin. Second, turn away from those things. And, third, turn toward God and his grace**. The Bible says, "Let us test and examine our ways.

There are two things to remember here: (1) God's mercy is indeed infinite, and (2) true repentance means forsaking your sins. On the one hand, because of the infinite Atonement of Jesus Christ, **repentance is available to everyone, even those who have made the same mistakes many times.**

True repentance leads a person to say, "I have sinned" and prove it with a 180-degree change of their direction. Repentance requires true brokenness. **Repentance is NOT asking the Lord for forgiveness with the intent to sin again**. Repentance is an honest, regretful acknowledgment of sin with commitment to change. **And live so that others see your life, hear your word, observe your works, and they don't say anything about you**. They give glory to God. That is a radically different way to live. It's a revolutionary way to live. It's the exact opposite of pride. The psalmist vows to use God's Word to shine a light on his path. He's not suggesting that God's Word shines a light on the future, as if he could sneak a peek into events that would take place tomorrow or next year. He is saying that **God's Word helps him to understand right from wrong as he faces choices today**. Receive Jesus as the light on your path , the narrow road, let Him leads you, It is the spiritual and the divine light. We can't see our future, direction, or destination, but Jesus can. Like the lighthouse guided the ship, Jesus directs us toward God's light. **The light of Christ guides us through the darkness of sin, life, and struggle both spiritually and literally.John 8:12** Jesus applies the title to himself while debating with the Jews and states: I am the light of the world. Whoever follows me will never walk in darkness, but will have the light of life. The light is **your understanding that God is your Father, Jesus is your Savior, and your path is being led forward by the loving involvement of the Holy Spirit**. It is the awareness that what you were before knowing Jesus personally, and accepting His sacrifice, is nothing like what you are now. This leads us to 1 John 1:5, where we read "that God is light, and in him is no darkness at all." In describing God as light, **John is referring to His absolute moral purity and omniscience**. In other words, there is no moral defect, nor is there a lack of knowledge in God.

In the Bible, light has always been a symbol of **holiness, goodness, knowledge, wisdom, grace, hope, and God's revelation**. By contrast, darkness has been associated with evil, sin, and despair.

That is why we have to choose the road That is narrow to enter through Jesus, to become what we have to be.

They believed that we were "Spiritual Beings" having a human experience. They believed that we didn't need to take a step-by-step religious journey to connect with God, since we already had it. Being spiritual means **embracing our spiritual self, or soul**. They believed the soul was eternal and lived forever.

We are not human beings having a spiritual experience; we are spiritual beings having a human experience."

As your spiritual life deepens, **you may begin to feel a strong sense of compassion, empathy, kindness, and unconditional love for others**. You may find yourself also feeling more connected to animals and nature, and you may be more inclined to speak out for social justice and help those Including **the Spirit of the Lord, and the Spirits of wisdom, of understanding, of counsel, of might, of knowledge and of fear of the LORD**, here are represented the seven Spirits, which are before the throne of God. Walking with him **gives us assurance of his presence and power in our lives**. Our God is powerful and with him all things are possible. We can endure trials and heartache. Because of Christ's resurrection power in us, we can overcome. Thus **the upright person has a great respect for God and for his commandments**. The upright has a secure walk or lifestyle (Pr. 10:9), because that one is guided by integrity (Pr. 11:3), and avoids crooked paths (Phil. 2:15). **Things You Should Know**

1. To walk with God means to adopt a Godly lifestyle, meditating on God daily and living your life according to His will.
2. Walk with God by praying and studying the Bible. ...
3. Act out your faith by fellow shipping with other believers and obeying God's commands.

I failed many times to walk straight with God but I found grace and God completely turned my life around .

Hebrews 12:13-14

13 **Keep walking on straight paths, so that the lame foot may not be disabled, but instead be healed**. 14 Try to be at peace with everyone, and try to live a holy life, because no one will see the Lord without it.

Do not give up on yourself, while you heading towards the price, yes this is not a easy road, but it is a possible road.

Galatians 6:9

9 Let us not become weary in doing good, for at the proper time we will reap a harvest if we do not give up. **He promises to always be with us and never leave us nor forsake us**. (Deuteronomy

31:8). Even if our pain or our circumstances or our feelings lead us to believe He's no longer with us, we can choose to believe what God's Word tells us instead. He really does want to redeem your hard situation.

Joshua 1:9

"Be strong and courageous; do not be frightened and do not be dismayed, for the Lord your God is with you wherever you go."

God is our refuge and strength, an ever-present help in trouble. Therefore we will not fear, though the earth give way and the mountains fall into the heart of the sea, though its waters roar and foam and the mountains quake with their surging." This is a powerful Bible verse about strength and comfort. Jesus fell **three times** while carrying his cross to the place where he was crucified. The falls are marked as part of the Stations of the Cross, which many churches observe on Good Friday. In Luke 9:23, Jesus looks at his disciples and tells them, **"Whoever wants to be my disciple must deny themselves and take up their cross and follow me**. For whoever wants to save their life will lose it, but whoever loses their life for me will find it."

Taking up our cross means carrying around those places where we are vulnerable, places where we are maybe even exposed to embarrassment and shame. Those are not comfortable places, are they? They are places where we hurt. A call to bear one's cross as part of following Jesus, then, is **a call to be as submitted to Christ as the condemned criminal was to his death**. Therefore, when Jesus calls for self-denial and cross-bearing, he's claiming authority. Following Christ means disowning the self and giving allegiance to him instead.

The cross has significance as **a reminder of what Jesus did for**

us. It is a powerful symbol to remind us of the price paid for our redemption. Whether we wear it, display it, or just think about it, the cross can, and should, draw us nearer to the one who hung on it. It means **to lay our "ego strength" aside**. Taking up our cross means, instead, picking up those weaknesses that we so often try to run away from in life. Taking up our cross means carrying around those places where we are vulnerable, places where we are maybe even exposed to embarrassment and shame.

Through his death and resurrection Jesus tore down the power, meaning and significance of the cross, turning it wholeheartedly into something new, to become a symbol of life, honor and eternal victory.

So the cross for us as believers on this road, symbolize life in general. The cross, the principal symbol of the Christian religion, **recalling the Crucifixion of Jesus Christ and the redeeming benefits of his Passion and death**.

Turn to God:

Meaning:

But this is how God fulfilled what he had foretold through all the prophets, saying that his Messiah would suffer. 19 **Repent, then, and turn to God, so that your sins may be wiped out, that times of refreshing may come from the Lord, 20 and that he may send the Messiah, who has been appointed for you—even Jesus. To turn away from evil and to turn towards good**. To turn to God. We do this by confessing our sins, asking for forgiveness for them, and by turning away from them, not doing them again. This means that repentance is more than simply regretting our sins, more than being sad that we were caught doing something wrong.

Isaiah 55:6-7

7 Let the wicked forsake their ways and the unrighteous their thoughts. Let them turn to the LORD, and he will have mercy on them, and to our God, for he will freely pardon. The Lord knows each of us goes astray, and his nature is always to show mercy. Receive that mercy today and be transformed by it **through repentance and changing your life**. Through receiving the mercy of the Lord and allowing his trans formative work in your life, he is glorified in you and through you.

But the Bible also defines mercy beyond forgiveness and withholding punishment. **God shows his mercy for those who are suffering through healing, comfort, the alleviation of suffering and caring about those in distress**. He acts from compassion and acts with mercy.

Proverbs 28:13 – "No one who conceals transgressions will prosper, but one who confesses and forsakes them will obtain mercy." Isaiah 30:18 – "Therefore the Lord waits to be gracious to you; therefore he will rise up to show mercy to you. For the Lord is a God of justice; blessed are all those who wait for him."

God shows His mercy to **those who fear Him**, that is, to those who trust, worship, and obey Him, from generation to generation. Luke 1:50. Mary reaffirmed what the Lord said centuries before. The Lord delights in those who fear Him. Fear of God may refer to fear itself, but more often to **a sense of awe, and submission to, a deity**. People subscribing to popular monotheistic religions for instance, might fear Hell and divine judgment, or submit to God's omnipotence.

To fear the Lord is **to stand in awe of his majesty, power, wisdom, justice and mercy, especially in Christ – in his life, death and resurrection – that is, to have an exalted view of God**. To see God in all his glory and then respond to him appropriately.

To humble ourselves before him. To adore him. **Psalms 34:9**

9 Fear the LORD, you his holy people, for those who fear him lack nothing.

There is a blessing to the fear of God on this narrow road.

The blessing

How is the one who fears the LORD blessed? First, **fearing the Lord will give you wisdom** (Psalm 111:10). Second, fearing the Lord will keep you from sin (Exodus 20:20).

And third, fearing the Lord will motivate you in evangelism (2 Corinthians 5:11).

For when we see God for who he is as the sovereign and almighty God, and we recognize the salvation that he offers to each one of us through Jesus Christ, then we will respond by standing in awe of Him and offering our lives in worship. That is what it means to fear God. They are not the same thing. The terror of God describes the reaction of persons who come into God's unmitigated presence who do not know God's nature. The fear of God describes the posture of persons who know the enormity of God's holiness and yet trust in the extravagance of God's goodness. **To fear the Lord leads us to respect Him and His laws**. We learn how we are to act and even what we should say by fearing the Lord. This fear, or reverence, makes us think before we act or speak. As we gain knowledge, we gain wisdom.

Walking in the fear of the Lord is **to love Him so much that we are afraid to be away from Him**. We love Him and value His presence above all. Out of reverence for Him, we choose to love what He loves and hate what He hates. **Hate the sin and not the sinner is a precept which, though easy enough to understand, is rarely practiced, and that is why the poison of hatred spreads in the world**...

Proverbs 8:13 "**The fear of the LORD is to hate evil: pride,**

and arrogance, and the evil way, and the forward mouth, do I
hate."

We as Christians must turn away from sin we to easy Fall for
the devil and his mark, Listen to this, "**You shall not make
gashes in your flesh for the dead, or incise any marks on
yourselves**." Historically, scholars have often understood this
as a warning against pagan practices of mourning. Leviticus
19:28

Repent.

Matthew 10:28) "God loves the sinner, but He hates the sin,"
suggests that **God doesn't punish sinners, because it directs
His anger away from the sinner**.

But we must do right to God by repentance and stop sinning.

Because sin can move your into the wrong direction.

The answer is **if you practice sin, you WILL NOT go to heaven**.
You will go to hell to spend an eternity of torment away from
God's presence and goodness and glory. "Or do you not know
that the unrighteous will not inherit the kingdom of God? Unless
you turn away from your sin.

And so I tell you, every kind of sin and slander can be forgiven,
but **blasphemy against the Spirit** will not be forgiven. Anyone
who speaks a word against the Son of Man will be forgiven, but
anyone who speaks against the Holy Spirit will not be forgiven,
either in this age or in the age to come (Matthew 12:31–32).

Look at that that urge of God, All sins shall be forgiven, except
the **sin against the Holy Ghost**; for Jesus will save all except
the sons of perdition. What must a man do to commit the
unpardonable sin? He must receive the Holy Ghost, have the
heavens opened unto him, and know God, and then sin against
him. want to assure you that for all those in Christ, the answer
to this question is a resounding "Yes!" **Yes, God will forgive all**

of your sins. Even the ones that have plagued you the longest and consumed you the most. God's forgiveness does not depend in the slightest degree on what you do or not do.

There are two things to remember here: (1) **God's mercy is indeed infinite**, and (2) true repentance means forsaking your sins. On the one hand, because of the infinite Atonement of Jesus Christ, repentance is available to everyone.

The Sinner's Prayer:

"Heavenly Father, I know that I am a sinner and that I deserve to go to hell. I believe that Jesus Christ died on the cross for my sins. I do now receive him as my Lord and personal Savior.

In many church settings, **the prayer itself is considered the entirety and assurance of salvation**. In other words, as long as someone prays the right words of the "Sinner's Prayer" and "really means it," he can rest assured that he is saved.

Pray This Prayer for Salvation:

Lord, I admit I am a sinner. I need and want Your forgiveness. I accept Your death as the penalty for my sin, and recognize that Your mercy and grace is a gift You offer to me because of Your great love, not based on anything I have done. Cleanse me and make me Your child.

For instance, Jesus asks for harvest workers (Matthew 9:37-38) and for strength in the midst of temptation (Matthew 26:40-41), for faith and strength of his chosen ones (Luke 22:31-32), and for the sanctification and protection of these chosen ones when he is gone (John 17:11–26).

Can you be saved without saying the Sinners prayer?

The answer is no. **We are not saved by saying particular words or by praying a particular prayer**. We are saved by grace alone through faith alone in Christ alone.

We as Christians have to believe and pray the prayer everyday to find His grace to work for us.

MY DAILY PRAYER :

Dear Lord Jesus, I know that I am a sinner, and I ask for Your forgiveness. I believe You died for my sins and rose from the dead. I turn from my sins and invite You to come into my heart and life. I want to trust and follow You as my Lord and Savior.

When John says in 1 John 3:6 that, "no one who abides in him keeps on sinning," he means that **no one who practices sin abides in God**. So if we habitually, continually, constantly, joyfully and frequently practice any sin, we are not children of God. Christ died for our sins, rose again so that we might be justified in union with him, and is now pleading our case before the Father on the basis of his work for us. **His intercession can save us to the uttermost because his intercession is rooted in his death and resurrection. Confess to God through Jesus Christ, that you are a sinner in need of forgiveness and ask Him to cleanse you.** Understand that Jesus is the source of your forgiveness. Trust in Jesus by faith that His work on the cross saves, frees, and forgives you. Receive the indwelling of the Holy Spirit, who will guide and teach you.

Salvation of precious souls.

Lord Jesus, I confess my sins and ask for your forgiveness. Please come into my heart as my Lord and Savior. Take complete control of my life and help me to walk in Your footsteps daily by the power of the Holy Spirit. Thank you Lord for saving me and for answering my prayer.

The salvation of the spirit is based on the finished work of our Savior Jesus Christ at Calvary - **the spirit is saved simply by believing on the Lord Jesus Christ**. While the spirit is saved by faith in Christ, the soul is being saved based upon the faithfulness of the believer.

How to Accept Christ

1. Acknowledge that you are a sinner.
2. Confess your sins to God.
3. Ask God to forgive you of your sins.
4. Ask God to come into your heart.
5. Accept Him as Lord and Savior of your life.

Prayer for Protection:

"Lord, we pray for the safety and protection of our family members. Keep us safe from harm and lead us in the paths of righteousness. Shield us from any danger and guide us through life's challenges." A Prayer for Gratitude:

"Dear God, we thank you for the gift of family.

Amen.

The peace of God on the journey:

True peace of mind comes from God, rather than from

anyone or anything in the world (John 14:27). Not only does God give people peace, but "he himself is our peace" (Ephesians 2:14). That kind of peace of mind is completely reliable in any circumstances. You may have heard of, or read, the Bible verses from Philippians 4:6-7: Do not be anxious about anything, but in every situation, by prayer and petition, with thanksgiving, present your requests to God. And **the peace of God, which transcends all understanding, will guard your hearts and your minds in Christ Jesus.**

Peace of mind comes from our Master Jesus. He is the master at putting our mind at ease with His eternal perspective. It is trust in Him that gives us tranquil thoughts. Without His peace we worry and fret.

Ways to have the Peace of God Wrap Up

1. Pray.
2. Be grateful.
3. Right Thinking.
4. Obedience.
5. Trust God.

The only way we can obtain peace of mind is **when this knowl-edge and these promises become ours as we read and respond with faith and obedience to the word of God**. In other words you could say, "The peace of God comes into your heart when the God of peace is on your mind through His word." Peace is **knowing that the Lord of the universe is by your side and resting in that**. It's not just knowing, but it is also living it out. Peace is sitting in comfort and knowing that God is next to your side no matter what.

There are this three tipes of peace, that we as Christian

believers need to master on our path.

Peace with God is a gift of the Lord Jesus Christ. Peace within oneself is a fruit of the Holy Spirit. And peace between people is a work of righteousness. God-Given Peace, is not any peace , it is pure and true, and it give us the faith,

"Do not be anxious about anything,

Christians can expect to find inner peace in and through **living out their vocation as disciples of Jesus Christ and directing their lives towards the following of his teaching**. Our minds will never be peaceful when **we cannot let go of the past**. If we carry past events with us all the time, we burden ourselves with luggage that increases in weight every day. The problem is: we cannot change the past.

The question is can we realy live a peaceful life at all? Yes

1. Focus on the present. Focus on the present moment by thinking about your five senses. ...
2. Go outside every day. ...
3. Remove clutter and keep your space organized. ...
4. Avoid judgment. ...
5. Practice gratitude. ...
6. Spend quality time with loved ones.

We can **turn our heart to Him and pray, call on His name, sing to Him, or simply talk to Him**. Through our fellowship with Him, God becomes our true inner peace and rest, the much-needed antidote to our easily troubled soul. This is only possible **because we have been made right with God, through faith in Jesus Christ**. "We have peace with God because of what Jesus Christ our Lord has done for us," (Romans 5:1). If only we can let go and trust God. Then we'll have peace.

Psalm 29:11

"The Lord gives strength to his people, and the Lord blesses his people with peace."

Peace is like a fruit, **No branch can bear fruit by itself; it must remain in the vine**. Neither can you bear fruit unless you remain in me. "I am the vine; you are the branches. If a man remains in me and I in him, he will bear much fruit; apart from me you can do nothing. For us to bear the fruit of the Spirit, we must **live in the Spirit and walk in the Spirit**. For the Spirit to "live in us" is the same as for Him to "dwell in us." The Spirit lives (or dwells) in us through the Word of God, the Bible. Paul said, "Let the word of Christ dwell in you richly..." (Colossians 3:16). It is just where we can find that inner peace He is talking about to us. It is found in the fullness of the Holy Spirit.

Jesus said, "Live in me. **Make your home in me just as I do in you**. In the same way that a branch can't bear grapes by itself but only by being joined to the vine, you can't bear fruit unless you are joined with me. I am the Vine, you are the branches. Yes, Christian converts are like fruit harvested for God. So you see, according to Jesus, **God wants us to bear fruit**. And the fruit he wants is the fruit of Christian character, Christian conduct, and Christian converts. Jesus not only tells us what God wants from us, he also describes what God does for. us. Listen to this, that if we abide in Him, **if our hearts are fixed on Him and we are filling our minds and heart with His** Word we will bear fruit. We will have peace.

If we not have the Peace of God in our hearts and if we not bare the good fruits than we actually do have a big problem, so what will happen to us not producing , On the narrow road is it possible, If anyone does not abide in me **he is thrown away like a branch and withers; and the branches are gathered, thrown into the fire, and burned**.

The 12 Fruits are: **Charity, Joy, Peace, Patience, Kindness, Goodness, Generosity, Gentleness, Faithfulness, Modesty, Self-Control, & Chastity**.

Let us work , to produce fruit , and share it with one another in Love, with our friends and families and the world around us. It is our work to keep God's people together and show them which way to go. That all may enter eternity.

Jesus said:

In Me you may have peace (John 16:33)

I have told you these things, so that in me you may have peace. In this world you will have trouble. But take heart!

This road is not easy,

Romans 8:18

"For I consider that the sufferings of this present time are not worth comparing with the glory that is to be revealed to us." These verses remind us that we are not alone and that we have the strength to overcome even the toughest challenges! Finally, be strong in the Lord and in his mighty power." These verses remind us that no matter how weak we may feel, God is always with us, providing us with the strength and support we need to endure and overcome any obstacle. **God is our refuge and strength, an ever-present help in trouble**. Therefore we will not fear, though the earth give way and the mountains fall into the heart of the sea, though its waters roar and foam and the mountains quake with their surging." This is a powerful Bible verse about strength and comfort.My flesh and my heart may fail, but God is the strength of my heart and my portion forever." Nehemiah 8:10—"Do not grieve, for the joy of the Lord is your strength." Psalm 46:5—"God is within her, she will not fall; God will help her at break of day."

Calm a troubled mind and spirit.

1. Talk with God. Set aside time to really have a conversation. ...
2. Practice gratitude. Think about times you've felt blessed. ...
3. Evaluate expectations. Sometimes our greatest stress comes when life doesn't turn out the way we planned. ...
4. Take a break. Take several slow, deep breaths. ...

Matthew 11:28-30

"Come to me, all you that are weary and are carrying heavy burdens, and I will give you rest. Take my yoke upon you, and learn from me; for I am gentle and humble in heart, and you will find rest for your souls. For my yoke is easy, and my burden is light."

Prayer for strength:

Dear God, please give me strength when I am weak, love when I feel forsaken, courage when I am afraid, wisdom when I feel foolish, comfort when I am alone, hope when I feel rejected, and peace when I am in turmoil. Amen.

God of all comfort, our very present help in trouble, be near to me. Look on me with the eyes of your mercy; comfort me with a sense of your presence; preserve me from the enemy; and give me patience in my affliction. Restore me to health, and lead me to your eternal glory; through Jesus Christ our Lord. Amen.

1. Seek Truth in Scripture.
2. Confess Unbelief. Be honest. ...
3. Share Your Concerns With Your Community.
4. Remember God and Spend Time With Him. God is bigger than your circumstances. ...
5. Look for Things to Be Grateful For.
6. Walk in the Holy Spirit. ...
7. Pray honestly. God already knows how you really feel, and what you really think (Hebrews 4:12-13). ...
8. Find people who love Him. ...
9. Be vulnerable. ...
10. Turn to Scripture. ...
11. Remember the times He has been faithful. ...
12. Do not lose heart.

Positive energies, **Connecting with friends and family** when you're going through tough times can help ease stress, boost your mood, and make sense of all the change and disruption. Instead of feeling like you're facing your problems alone, you can draw strength and build resilience from having others to lean on.

Paul wrote to Corinth: "For the sake of Christ, then, I am content with weaknesses, insults, hardships, persecutions, and calamities. For when I am weak, then I am strong" (**2**

Corinthians 12:10).

Psalm 18:1–5

"I love you, Lord, my strength. "The Lord is my rock, my fortress and my deliverer; my God is my rock, in whom I take refuge, my shield and the horn of my salvation, my stronghold. "I called to the Lord, who is worthy of praise, and I have been saved from my enemies.

Spiritual Disciplines to Help Grow Your Walk With God

1. Read Your Bible. The Bible is compelling, isn't it? ...
2. Pray. Always. ...
3. Fast. Fasting puts us in the place of trusting God to fulfill our lives, and yes, that includes the physical feeling of hunger. ...
4. Worship. ...
5. Journal.

The LORD makes firm the steps of the one who delights in him; though he may stumble, he will not fall, for the LORD upholds him with his hand." The Good News: Struggles are part of life, but **as long as God is in your life, he will provide comfort and strength.**

Try not to overthink.
Relaxing and calming exercises

1. Take a break. Focus on your breathing. Listen to music.
2. Spend some time in nature. Try active relaxation. Think of

somewhere else.

3. Try guided meditation. Get creative.

How to Tap into Your Spiritual Energy

1. 1) Daily, morning meditation. Begin your day with a meditation practice. ...
2. 2) Take altruistic action within the community. ...
3. 3) Get a daily dose of nature. ...
4. 4) Surround yourself in music. ...
5. 5) Listen to your gut. ...
6. 6) Support your mind and body. ...
7. 7) Appreciate what you have. ...
8. 8) Accept others.

Tips on How to Hear from God

1. Position yourself close to God. Samuel set his bed up in the temple, "where the ark of God was" (v. ...
2. Find a place of regular service to God. In v. ...
3. Listen for God's voice. ...
4. When God calls, respond eagerly. ...
5. When God speaks, obey Him. ...
6. Read and study the Word of God.

You can **pray about it**; if we ask God to lead us toward whatever gifts He has given us, he can make it clearer to us. Some churches offer spiritual gifts classes to help you discover yours. Ask a leader at your church if this is something they offer. Beloved

God, I thank you because I know that you hear my cry, in the day of my distress you are at my side, you do not forsake me and you lift me up before my enemies. I thank you for caring also to have mercy on us human beings, mere sinners.

My prayer:
   Lord, lift me up for Your blessings today. I pray that you will anoint me with strength and self care today, tomorrow, and always. I pray that You will grace me with patience and wisdom. I invite you into my life, Jesus. I accept you as my Lord, God and Savior. Heal me, change me, strengthen me in body, soul, and spirit. Come Lord Jesus, cover me with your Precious Blood, and fill me with your Holy Spirit.
   Amen.

My advise and encouragement to you:
   Instead of repeating things you worry about in your mind, you can repeat God's Word through meditation. Christian meditation is simply focusing on God's Word and thinking about it deeply. It's also a proven way to decrease stress and increase peace. **Keep Talking to God**. Just because God seems silent doesn't mean you should doubt Him or stop praying. God's silence isn't a license for us to turn our backs on Him. Instead, it's an invitation to press forward and seek Him even more diligently. **Every day, you can offer up your worries to God in prayer. Hand them over to him and trust him to take care of those matters**. Do this as many times as needed to surrender to God, and you'll experience God's perfect peace. Stay in the present moment.

These seven things are simple but meaningful ways we can

demonstrate our love and appreciation for God that will speak volumes to Him personally: **giving Him praise, praying to Him, reading the Bible, loving those around us, tithing, fasting, and being hopeful**. We can outline the process of rebuilding trust in four steps:

(1) **admit and repent,**
(2) **define and exhibit trustworthy actions,**
(3) **recognize and encourage trustworthy actions, and**
(4) **trust in God**.

God is present **amid the bad times as well as the good**. He is always faithful. God wants you to go to Him with your circumstances. He also wants you to come to Him simply to spend time with Him. For when I am weak, then I am strong" (**2 Corinthians 12:9-10**). Paul is strong when he is weak because when he is weak, God's grace is most powerful.

GOD BLESS

Shane Marquin van Rooyen